RAINBOWS, UNICORNS, AND TRIANGLES

OF RELATED INTEREST

The Big Book of Pride Flags
Illustrated by Jem Milton
ISBN 978 1 83997 258 4
eISBN 978 1 83997 259 1

Me and My Dysphoria Monster
An Empowering Story to Help
Children Cope with Gender Dysphoria
Laura Kate Dale
Illustrated by Ang Hui Qing
ISBN 978 1 83997 092 4
eISBN 978 1 83997 093 1

Gender Heroes
25 Amazing Transgender, Non-
Binary and Genderqueer Trailblazers
from Past and Present!
Illustrated by Filipa Namorado
ISBN 978 1 83997 325 3
eISBN 978 1 83997 326 0

Sylvia and Marsha Start
a Revolution!
The Story of the Trans Women of
Color Who Made LGBTQ+ History
Joy Michael Ellison
Illustrated by Teshika Silver
ISBN 978 1 78775 530 7
eISBN 978 1 78775 531 4

First published in Great Britain in 2024 by Jessica Kingsley Publishers
An imprint of John Murray Press

1

Copyright © Jessica Kingsley Publishers 2024
Illustration copyright © Jem Milton 2024

The fonts, layout, and overall design of this book have been prepared according to dyslexia-friendly principles. At Jessica Kingsley Publishers we aim to make our books' content accessible to as many readers as possible.

A CIP catalogue record for this title is available from the British Library and the Library of Congress

ISBN 978 1 80501 041 8
eISBN 978 1 80501 044 9

Printed and bound in China by Leo Paper Products Ltd

Jessica Kingsley Publishers' policy is to use papers that are natural, renewable and recyclable products and made from wood grown in sustainable forests. The logging and manufacturing processes are expected to conform to the environmental regulations of the country of origin.

Jessica Kingsley Publishers
Carmelite House
50 Victoria Embankment
London EC4Y 0DZ

www.jkp.com

John Murray Press
Part of Hodder & Stoughton Limited
An Hachette UK Company

RAINBOWS UNICORNS & TRIANGLES

Queer Symbols Throughout History

Illustrated by Jem Milton

Jessica Kingsley Publishers
London and Philadelphia

Queer Symbols

Throughout history, LGBTQIA2s+ people could not always be open about their lives. At various times, queer people used different symbols to communicate who they were to each other. Other symbols were used to show pride. Some symbols were used to persecute queer people.

This book explains some of these symbols.

Green Carnations

In 19th-century England, green was a symbol of homosexual love. The green carnation, worn on the lapel, was popularized by the Irish poet and playwright Oscar Wilde, who was open about being a gay man.

Many gay men of the time picked up on this and wore the green carnation to secretly signal their homosexuality.

Violets

A poem by Sappho, the lesbian poet of ancient Greece, talked about women who loved one another wearing crowns of violets. Because of this poem, the violet became a symbol of lesbian love.

In the 1920s, if a woman loved another woman as more than friends, it was common to send her a bouquet with violets in it.

Polari

In the 1920s, because of anti-gay laws in the UK, queer people used a type of slang called Polari to show each other that they were safe. Polari is a mix of languages like French and Italian, sailor slang, and rhyming slang.

Words used in Polari included "naff" (boring or drab), "zhoosh" (to stylize or smarten up), "strides" (trousers), and phrases like "So bona to vada you!" (So good to see you!).

This secret language helped many gay men survive a time that was very dangerous for them.

Camp

NAFF!

Dish!

Unicorns

There are many ways in which the unicorn became a symbol of gay pride. The mythical unicorn is said to represent lives lived outside heterosexuality.

The unicorn is also an animal that is quite fabulous, something the LGBTQIA2s+ community is often fond of!

Lavender Rhino

Used in a public advertising campaign in the 1970s by the LGBTQIA2s+ group Gay Media Action-Advertising, the rhinoceros symbolized the misunderstood, which many queer people identified with. The lavender purple color was made by mixing pink and blue.

A full-sized papier mâché purple rhino appeared in the Boston Pride parade in 1974.

Purple Hand

During a peaceful LGBTQIA2s+ protest in the 1960s, employees of a newspaper threw ink on the protestors' heads from an office above them. The protestors used it to make purple handprints and paint queer pride slogans on the buildings around them.

The purple handprints stayed on the buildings for some time. They became a symbol of resistance for the queer community.

Lambda

Lambda is the 11th letter of the Greek alphabet, which symbolized unity under oppression to the Spartans. It was chosen as a symbol for gay and lesbian rights by the Gay Activists Alliance in the 1970s, and the International Gay Rights Congress in 1974.

The word "Lambda" is currently used in an LGBTQIA2s+ legal organization, a queer book awards organization, and several queer college social clubs around the world.

Labrys

This double-edged axe was adopted as a symbol of lesbian pride in the 1970s. The symbol stands for strength. It was also the symbol for warrior women in Ancient Greece. At other points in history, it signified the power of women and goddesses.

Pink & Black Triangles

During World War II, queer people were among some of the most discriminated-against groups in Germany. Gay men were forced to wear pink triangle badges on their arms. Lesbian women were forced to wear black ones.

These symbols were used by the repressive government of Nazi Germany to differentiate gay and lesbian people, and single them out for horrible treatment.

The pink triangle was later reclaimed as a symbol of gay pride while standing against persecution.

Rainbows

American artist and activist Gilbert Baker's Rainbow Flag is a well-known symbol of gay pride. Some people think that he created this pride symbol to hint at Judy Garland singing "Somewhere Over the Rainbow" in *The Wizard of Oz*, as Garland was one of the first gay icons.

The flag has since been updated to be more inclusive of the various LGBTQIA2S+ identities. The rainbow is still a symbol of queer pride.

Ace Playing Cards

This symbol came to stand for asexuality because "asexual" is commonly shortened to "ace". All the ace cards can represent asexuality and its many variations. The Asexuality Visibility and Education Network frequently discusses which of the ace identities are which suit's ace card.

Black Ring

A plain black ring worn on the middle finger of the right hand is a very subtle way of signaling asexuality. First discussed on the Asexuality Visibility and Education Network message boards in 2005, this subtle symbol of one's identity is a bit like a secret handshake for ace people.

Other people of various sexual identities sometimes use the black ring as a symbol too. Out of respect for asexual identities, they do not wear it on the middle finger of the right hand.

Red Tie / Bow Tie

In New York City in the early 20th century, a red bow tie or a red tie was often worn as a "flag," or a signal from one gay man to another that they identified as part of the queer community. It was a successor to the green carnation and served the same purpose.

Later, the color red would become linked to the fight against HIV and AIDS.

Prop 8 & the White Knot

In 2008, activist Frank Voci created the white knot as a symbol of gay marriage after laws were passed in California (Proposition 8) that were intended to ban gay marriage. White is commonly used to symbolize purity and so is often used in wedding ceremonies.

The knot was a play on "tying the knot," another way of saying "getting married." The laws were later overturned, and in June 2015 gay marriage became legal across the United States.

Questions for Discussion

- Why would some people have to be so secretive about who they are and how they live their lives?

- In what ways did these symbols help keep LGBTQIA2s+ people safe?

- In what ways can greater visibility for a marginalized population be a good thing?

- In what ways can it be a dangerous thing?

- Some of these symbols were used to persecute the people who had to wear them but were "reclaimed" as symbols of pride. How do you think this helped people who reclaimed them?

- Why is it important to choose how and when you decide to reveal a part of your life to the public, but still have ways that other people like you can identify you as one of them?

- If you had to create a secret symbol for people who have something in common with you, what would it look like?